TRIANGLE CARD

STAR CARD

The MEDITATION KIT

Tara Ward

ARCTURUS

First published in Great Britain by
Arcturus Publishing Limited
First Floor
1-7 Shand Street
London
SE1 2ES

For Bookmart Limited
Desford Road
Enderby
Leicester LE9 5AD
This edition published 2000

Printed and bound in Czech Republik
603655101
Design by Zeta Fitzpatrick @ Moo
Illustrations by Tania Field
Edited by Emma Hayley

© Arcturus Publishing Limited

ISBN 1 84193 026 1

CONTENTS

INTRODUCTION

Many people find the word meditation rather daunting. Do you find it a warm, natural word or does it conjure up an image for you of someone sitting cross-legged in a dimly-lit room, a strange smile on their face, surrounded by incense and candles, with animal noises wailing in the background – somewhat like the image below?

Some forms of meditation do indeed encompass the sorts of things shown here, BUT – and this is a BIG "but" – meditation doesn't have to involve all that to be effective. Meditation is actually described in a number of dictionaries as "...deep reflection". That seems a much more helpful image! It's simply to think about something in a deep and meaningful way. In fact, most of us involve ourselves in "mini meditations" all the time.

How often do you daydream about someone or something? Do you sit down to relax and suddenly find that time has passed quicker than you expected and yet you weren't doing anything in particular and you weren't asleep? When you're on a bus or train and you suddenly reach your destination, have you sometimes come back to "reality" with a jolt and realised that your thoughts were elsewhere, even if you can't remember quite what you were thinking about? These are good examples of little meditations, without you even trying!

This kit is about helping you to discover that meditation, far from being unnerving and difficult, is actually a very simple, natural process that we can learn easily. It's also fun!

In fact, let's try an experiment straight away. Open the envelope at the back of this kit and find the Window Card. Prop it up in front of you (don't hold it as this can make your arms ache). Read through the exercise on the next page and then when you're ready, close your eyes and remember to relax and breathe deeply. Then reopen your eyes and look at the Window Card, allowing your thoughts to spiral as demonstrated in the exercise. Focus purely on the Window Card.

THE MEDITATION KIT

Window Card – Find this card at the back of the kit

8

INTRODUCTION

LOOKING OUT OF THE WINDOW

First of all, take a moment to relax by taking a few good, deep breaths and settling your body comfortably. Give yourself time to do this. There's no rush.

Now look at the Window Card. Gaze at the open window and imagine you are actually in front of it, looking out through it. Don't strain or stare too hard. Soften your gaze, as if your eyes were half-closed and let the image blur a little in front of you. What is through that open window? What is out there, waiting for you to explore? Whatever it is, it is exciting and appealing.

If you feel like it, let your thoughts waft out through the open window and float outwards and upwards. What can you see? What are you feeling? Enjoy the pleasurable, relaxing experience of letting your thoughts soar outwards and upwards, free from normal every-day restrictions.

Don't worry at this stage where your thoughts and sensations lead you. It doesn't matter at all, so long as you feel calm and comfortable. Drift lazily in this new state of relaxation and freedom.

Let yourself fly free for a few moments and then bring yourself back down to where you are now. Take your focus away from the Window Card and look at another object around you.

Remember what time of the day it is. Remember what day of the week it is, what year you are in. Feel how heavy your body suddenly feels. Make sure you give yourself a few minutes to "come back to earth" before you get up again.

Did that feel liberating or did nothing happen for you? It doesn't matter if you felt very little because there are certain basic steps to lead you into meditation and you may need to follow those to fully experience the sense of release which comes with meditating. If you did feel something and had the sensation of your thoughts soaring outwards, congratulations! You are well on your way.

So, meditation involves the experience of releasing yourself from the pressures and restrictions of every-day life. That sounds pretty relaxing and enjoyable, doesn't it? However, meditation does even more than this.

The process of meditation also affords you the chance to take a journey (figuratively speaking) to somewhere you will probably never have been before. Many meditators have tried to explain this "place" you go to and it always ends up being difficult to describe – for each person the experience is very personal and different. A simple way to put it is that meditation is about finding your own private sanctuary of peace and stillness.

This sanctuary is where you can totally relax and be yourself, free from outside pressures and stresses. You don't have to be

THE MEDITATION KIT

anything other than who you really are. How often do you put on faces for the outside world, trying to be what other people want you to be, trying to please everyone at once irrespective of how you are really feeling, trying to be strong and supportive for others, trying to get it right all the time? In meditation, you get rid of all your "faces". You simply become yourself. Pure, unadulterated "you".

Does the thought of that suddenly make you feel vulnerable? You needn't worry because the joy of meditation is that it is always utterly personal and private. No one need ever know what you are doing or how you are feeling during meditation. It is your time to be completely "you" in a perfectly safe environment, away from everyone and everything, to fully relax. And, of course, you can have all your "faces" back at the end of the meditation! Or you may decide that you don't need some of those faces and you may choose to let them go. You decide for yourself through the meditation process.

Wouldn't you say that there could be a lot of benefits from having this respite from daily pressures? How might going into this private world of discovering who you really are, help you personally? After all, if you're thinking of giving up some of your free time to meditate, you want to know what's in it for you! Look at the following list.

BEFORE MEDITATION

• I feel under pressure

• I can wake up after a night's sleep and still feel tired

• I find it difficult to relax

• I can't stop thoughts from racing around inside my head

• There isn't enough time in the day to do everything

• I don't know what I want in life

• I feel something is missing from my life

Do any of those statements above apply to you? At some time, most of us have felt stressed, upset or simply unsure about what we want in life. Are you someone who rushes around from one task to another, trying to cram so much into each day and feeling

INTRODUCTION

constantly under pressure to be the best that you can, whether it be the best partner, employee, child, parent or friend etc.? We often place untold pressures on ourselves, usually without realising it. Or have you reached a stage in your life where you feel "stuck", where you acknowledge that you have achieved a certain comfortable status in your life, where nothing is tangibly wrong or unpleasant, and yet you still feel somewhat empty and unsatisfied with your life without understanding why? Perhaps you feel there is more to life than the dull routine in which you presently find yourself and you want to try something new. Perhaps so many aspects of your life feel "wrong" to you that you don't know where to start.

Whatever stage you are at, meditation can enhance all areas of your life. So if you can relate to some of the statements above, let's see how you can be left feeling AFTER meditation.

Feel inner calm after meditation

AFTER MEDITATION

- I am calm and ready to face the tasks ahead of me
- I wake up in the morning feeling refreshed and rested
- I relax easily
- I can clear my head of nagging thoughts whenever I need to
- I accomplish what is necessary during each day
- I understand what I am capable of and what I am meant to do
- My life is happy and meaningful

THE MEDITATION KIT

Which sort of existence would you prefer to have? It's not a hard choice to make, is it? So are you now thinking that all this sounds far too easy? How can you go from one state into the other, without having to do a great deal of work in between?

The truth is that many eastern philosophies regard meditation as a natural, regular part of every day. It is considered as normal as eating and sleeping and breathing – and no one in the western world has trouble with those three activities! We know we couldn't survive without them. Yet somehow meditation is still seen by many of us as something complementary, rather than essential.

Of course this attitude is rapidly changing as more and more westerners are acknowledging that this thing called meditation, far from being a strange ritual, is in fact a wonderfully natural and richly rewarding technique that everyone can learn. We're just rediscovering what our eastern counterparts have already known for years.

So is meditation really that easy? What is actually involved? Meditation is basically the withdrawing of your senses from the outside, everyday world into a quiet, internal one, where you linger in a state of peace and stillness. Shutting off from everyday life, consciously choosing to close out the world around you for a

period of time might sound a hard state to accomplish. Meditation does require a certain degree of focus, it's true, and this is where many people start to feel daunted, offering excuses such as "ah, well, my concentration's never been any good". So now consider this.

If you choose to watch a film or read a book, these are actions that require an enormous amount of concentration, aren't they? Yet do you sit down in the cinema or pick up a good book and immediately think, "Oh dear, I guess I'll have to concentrate on this now." Most people simply look forward to being transported into another realm for a period of time. The process of losing yourself into another world is a deeply relaxing and very pleasurable pastime. Meditation is very similar to reading or watching a film. The only difference is that we're more likely to approach meditation with trepidation and uncertainty because we're ignorant of what it really entails and we may have preconceived ideas about how hard it might be. In other words, we ourselves create problems and blocks when they don't even exist!

There is only one way to prove that meditation is easy and fun – by doing it! So let's look at how we prepare for this new adventure.

1. GETTING READY

There are a few things you will always want to do before you start meditating – these are simple and common-sense actions which you'll get used to following automatically.

Then there are also some additional tools that you can use to make meditation easier in the beginning. These are things with which you can experiment to see what works best for you. After all, you want meditating to be fun and enjoyable. It isn't something you want to get over with as soon as possible. Meditation is a pleasurable pastime that you can look forward to and make into a special, nurturing experience.

So let's start with the actions you always want to take before meditating. Here's the basic list:

MEDITATION "MUSTS"

• A quiet, undisturbed location (lock door if necessary)

• Wear loose, comfortable clothing

• Be alcohol and drug free

• Have a glass of mineral water within easy reach of you

• Have your chosen meditation card propped up in front of you

• Find a comfortable position in which to sit / lie completely still

• Remember to breathe!!!

All these may seem fairly obvious actions to take but they are also all very important. It is essential that you are alone and not disturbed during meditation. It's easy to go into deep states of relaxation and you need to gently bring yourself back into your normal, everyday world as you finish meditating. If you are suddenly interrupted by someone bursting into the room, it can really unnerve you and stop you from relaxing so easily the next time. So do make sure you lock the door and, if necessary, even put up a sign saying: "Don't Disturb – Meditating!"

Loose, comfortable clothing is important because meditating is all about breathing deeply and evenly. That's hard to do if you have a tight collar around your neck or a waistband restricting your stomach area. You're going to be on your own, so you can undo those buttons and zippers and let your body have a chance to relax fully.

Being alcohol and drug free is equally important. Meditation is about freeing the mind – drugs and alcohol distort the mind. If you mix the two states, you can end up having a very unpleasant experience. NEVER mix the two.

Often after meditation you can suddenly be aware that you feel thirsty. Your throat can feel dry. Always have a glass of water within easy reach, it means you can use that time of slowly sipping the water to gradually come back into your present day. You can just sit quietly and slowly reacquaint yourself with what you are soon going to get up and do. You should never rush to get up after meditation.

THE MEDITATION KIT

We are going to use the meditation cards in the back of this kit to help you sink into this wonderfully relaxing new world. You will want to have your chosen meditation card propped up in front of you, comfortably in your eye line. You don't want to be holding the card in your hands as that will rapidly become uncomfortable as you go deeper into your relaxed state.

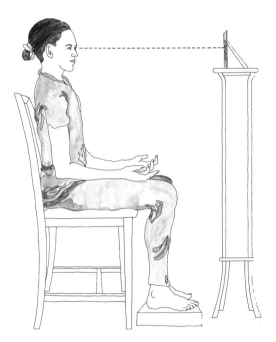

Place the meditation card in your eye line

An important issue is whether you want to sit or lie down during meditation. There is no firm rule on this but it is suggested that you try a comfortable sitting position first. The problem with lying down is that it is so tempting to drift off to sleep, instead of entering into a meditative state. Many people will tell you that the early stages of meditation are just so relaxing, all they want to do is sleep, particularly if they're feeling tired anyway. Whilst sleep

is a wonderfully regenerative action, it is not in any way related to meditation. The benefits of sleep and meditation are poles apart. To experience meditation and reap its rewards you need to be fully awake throughout the whole process.

Experienced meditators often choose to sit cross-legged on the floor but this is not essential. Do so only if this is comfortable for you. Your intention during meditation is to be completely still, physically. You therefore want to make yourself as comfortable as possible to help make this happen.

What is suggested initially is that you choose a comfortable upright chair and have your legs on the floor in front of you. It really helps if your body is in a comfortable alignment when you start meditating. If you look at the diagram on the next page you will see what is a good position to choose. If the chair is not padded, you might want to have a soft cushion on the seat and against the back.

You will see that the spine is upright, the hands resting comfortably in the lap (palms facing upwards is a good idea but not obligatory) and the feet are flat on the floor, preferably not encased in any footwear. The ideal is to have your thighs and lower legs at right angles to each other and the floor. This means there is no strain on your back. Try to find a chair which gives you this posture. You can always put your feet on a few books if your legs don't comfortably reach the floor. If you are tall, then try sitting on a few books to raise you up as necessary. If you suffer from any complaint and this is not a comfortable position for you, don't worry. Choose what feels right for you. If you are incapacitated in any way and can only lie flat for whatever reason, you can meditate that way. It just means you have to make that extra effort not to fall asleep! Remember that you want to remain physically motionless but mentally alert during your meditation.

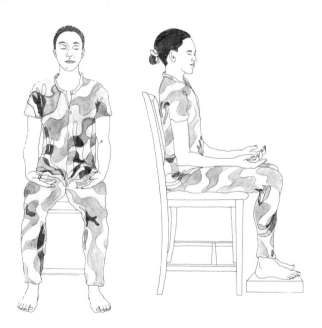

Sitting positions
Once you have done the above, the last stage is for you to simply close your eyes and concentrate on your breathing. Simple!

Remembering to breathe may sound like a very odd "must" for meditation but it is through focusing on the breath that we learn how to relax and then enter into a comfortable meditative state.

Acknowledging your breathing and how it is your very life force – we can not survive long without it – is your gateway into deeper states of relaxation.

In fact, focusing solely on your breathing is the only technique you need to develop to enter into meditation. That sounds too simple, doesn't it? Yet it's the truth. You may feel very cynical about that overtly simple statement. So now is the time for you to find out for yourself how true this is. When you are ready and have carried out the "musts" listed above, try the following:

BREATHING
Close your eyes and settle comfortably into your chosen position. Give a little wriggle if you feel uncomfortable.

Now, simply start to think about your breathing. (Always breathe through your nose, unless it is physically impossible for you to do so). As you breathe in, feel the cool air coming in through your nostrils and going down through your throat and deep into your lungs. As you breathe out, focus on the air coming back up through your throat and gently out through your nose. Notice how much warmer it is now it has been heated by your body. Then feel the breath coming back in again. Feel it as you exhale. Keep this focus going. Don't force the breath or try to change it in anyway. Sometimes our breath is short, sometimes it's long. Don't try to turn it into anything different. Just notice how it feels.

THE MEDITATION KIT

You may notice your thoughts wandering after a moment onto something else. Gently pull them back to your breathing. Don't force anything. Just let yourself drift into this awareness of your breathing. Every time you find yourself going off elsewhere, take your thoughts back to the breath.

If it helps, you can use words to help focus your thoughts. Every time you breathe in, try saying "In". Every time you breathe out, try saying "Out". Continue. After a few minutes, you may realise that your breathing has slowed and become more even and deep. Don't force it, just let it be as it is. Keep coming back to the breath all the time.

After a few minutes more, slowly bring your thoughts back to your present time. What room are you sitting in? What time of day is it? Slowly, open your eyes. Focus on an object. What day of the week is it? What year is it? Notice how heavy your body feels as it rests in the chair. Wait until you are properly "back again" before you get up.

Were you surprised by how relaxed you felt when you opened your eyes again? If you felt it had no effect, then you weren't truly concentrating on your breathing. You may find that initially your thoughts just keep drifting off to other things constantly. You might have wanted to wriggle your body and felt uncomfortable. That is quite normal. All that matters is that you refocus onto your breathing without chiding yourself or being irritated. It may take

a few sessions before you start withdrawing from your everyday life and experiencing the peace and stillness within you.

After a little practice, it starts to feel so comforting and so pleasant, that you can do this little exercise constantly throughout the day. If you are suddenly feeling stressed, angry or irritated allow your eyes to close briefly and focus on your breath. It is amazing how unpleasant emotions can disperse so quickly when you allow them to be released by the breath. In fact, there are endless examples of when a moment's focus on your breathing during the day can accomplish great results. Here are just a few:

STOP TO BREATHE WHEN:

• you feel you just can't do something

• you are scared about some upcoming event or situation

• you are about to lose your temper

• you are frustrated over some issue or someone

• you feel someone is overwhelming you with their needs or expectations

• you are about to go to sleep

• you first get up in the morning

• you're on a crowded bus or train

• you are about to go into an important meeting

• you feel confused or uncertain over what to do

• you are about to make a major decision

• you feel that you might burst into tears

GETTING READY

In other words, pausing to take a few deep breaths can benefit you at any difficult moment in your life! Once you gradually get into the habit of remembering to think about your breathing, it becomes second nature just to stop and focus your thoughts for a minute. This simple act alone, done a dozen times through each day, can work miracles as far as relieving stress is concerned. If you can't quite believe it, try it yourself for just a few days or even a week. Below is a chart you can fill in. Notice the difference in how you respond to things when you give yourself that brief moment to stop and focus.

Getting into the habit of being more aware of your breathing on an everyday level will really help your meditation process because it's essential that you focus on your breathing every time you start meditating. After a while it becomes so easy and natural, that the process happens very quickly and you sink into a relaxed state without even being aware that you are doing so. You forget about your physical body and don't have any desire to wriggle about or scratch an itchy nose!

So you have now learnt very quickly and easily about what meditation requires. What are the other tools that may help your relaxation processes?

These can be quite basic things such as incense, soft lighting and music. None of these are essential but they can act as comforting aids that help you to relax, particularly in the early stages. You are realising that meditation is about withdrawing the senses. Carefully choosing the lighting, scents and sounds around you can help this process of withdrawing.

Situation & How I Felt	What Happened After Breathing

THE MEDITATION KIT

SCENTS

Let's look at scents first. Are you particularly sensitive to odours? Do you have a scent you like to have around you? You may already use incense or essential oils and know what you like. If not, take some time to visit your local health shop or a New Age shop and have a sniff through their incense sticks and oils. Is there one you find especially relaxing? Remember, this is about you unwinding, so don't opt for a scent that gives you an uplifting buzz! Many gift and candle shops now sell incense sticks separately which is an inexpensive way of finding out what you really like. Experiment and have different sticks in different rooms and at different times. Wait until you find an aroma that appeals to you before you try it during one of your meditations.

MUSIC

Music is also a very personal choice. You will want to avoid any music with lyrics as they will probably trigger off memories of everyday life. If you have nothing suitable, again spend some time in different shops and listen to the wealth of New Age music that is now available. Choose anything that feels relaxing and floaty to you. Some of the music you may find irritating or monotonous. It's important you spend time and really listen to the different types of music. Something very simple like the sounds of the sea, dolphins or harp music might be a good first choice. You decide what you like. If you have friends who already enjoy this sort of relaxing music, ask if they will lend you some so you can try it out in the privacy of your own place.

GETTING READY

LIGHTS

Soft lighting is also a good idea for meditation. Most people find it harder to relax in bright, harsh light. If it's daytime, try closing the curtains and put on a small side lamp. Does that feel more relaxing? You could put a lower watt bulb or even a coloured bulb in your lights while you meditate. Switch off the overhead light and try lighting a candle (making sure it is safe and secure). Candlelight can be particularly effective as its soft flickering flame can help lull you into a relaxed state. Many people use a candle flame as a focus to help their path into meditation. They simply focus on the flame flickering for a minute or two and then close their eyes and see the flame in their mind's eye. You can then still the flame and stop it flickering as you slowly sink into your relaxed state. Try this one day for yourself. Experiment and see what feels good for you.

You don't have to rush this process of getting ready to meditate. Meditation is about enjoying the whole process of relaxation. It is hard to instantly relax and transport yourself into another world. Be gentle and give yourself some time to adjust to this. Enjoy experimenting with different lighting, music and scents.

Once you have become familiar with the breathing technique and finished your experimenting, return to the Window Card again. Read through the exercise ("Returning to the Window") and then prop up the Window Card in front of you and drift away!

RETURNING TO THE WINDOW

Remember to close your eyes and focus on your breathing first. Don't rush this process. Then open your eyes and gaze at the Window Card. Slowly feel yourself being transported out through the window and into new realms. Is it easier this time because you are better prepared and relaxed? Let your thoughts float free. Let everything come and go in an easy flow.

Don't hang on to any thought, no matter what it may be. If you find yourself being taken to a lovely location such as a beach

THE MEDITATION KIT

or forest, enjoy the process but then let yourself float onward. Don't become totally immersed in any scenario which comes up but let yourself drift like the ebb and flow of the tide. Give yourself plenty of time to enjoy all these different, pleasurable sensations. Enjoy this new freedom.

When you are ready, ensure you come back again through the window and take time to bring yourself back to reality. Open your eyes and focus on a nearby object. Concentrate on how heavy and relaxed your body feels. Always remember to re-orientate yourself fully before you get up again.

You can return to the Window Card frequently. Each time you go out through the window you will probably find yourself being transported somewhere different. This is because meditation takes you to what is appropriate and nurturing for you at that particular moment in your life. Our needs vary from day to day, as do our meditations.

One last word on thought processes before we continue. Sometimes, you may find worrying or unpleasant thoughts entering your mind as you prepare to meditate or even during meditation. That's normal. We all have those thoughts at times in our life. Whenever that happens, let the thought drift away into nothingness. If it returns again, let it drift away again. Don't be angry or upset by the thought; it has a right to come into your mind, but you have

the absolute power to dismiss it. If it keeps returning, simply keep dismissing it, gently but firmly. If you get into the habit of doing this, it not only returns you into the deep state of relaxation, it also reaffirms to you that you are in control. Whatever thought comes into your head, you always have the power to get rid of it. Always let it drift away and never dwell on it.

If at any stage during your meditating, you reach a point where you keep having the unwanted thoughts and you are finding it difficult to get rid of them, then you might choose to create an image which enables you to wash them away. Below are some suggestions that you can try. Use them all at some point during your meditation and make a note of what works best for you.

GETTING RID OF UNWANTED THOUGHTS

- Wash the image away, using an imaginary shower or hose pipe. See the image actually disappear down the drainage hole.
- Create a fast-running brook or stream and toss the image into the water. See it swirling away into the distance.
- Imagine the unwanted image floating up high into the air, disappearing into nothingness. Imagine it tied to a helium balloon and then let the balloon go.
- Create a beautiful, roaring fire and throw the image into the flames. Watch it become nothing but ashes.
- Give the unwanted image an actual shape and then see it shrinking in your mind's eye. See it shrink to nothing.

20

• Create a big powerful creature such as a lion, elephant or whale. Have the image be eaten and totally absorbed by the massive animal. Realise that the unwanted image becomes powerless in such an enormous creature.

After trying all the above, why not then create your own personal image? Experiment with your own imagination and see where it leads you. It doesn't matter what you choose, as long as you find it effective.

Remember, meditation is always nurturing and comforting. It always leaves you calm, happy and at peace.

Now, when you feel ready, we'll start working with the other meditation cards in this kit and continue our journey into meditation.

The Meditation Cards

2. LET'S START!

Before you work with any of the meditation cards, it's important that you remember to follow the basic steps of preparation, and also to add any of the extra scents, lights or sounds you want. Incidentally, it is also fine if you end up deciding that you want silence, a plain light and no incense! You choose what is right for you.

Before concentrating on any of the meditation cards, you always want to focus on awareness of your breathing for at least two or three minutes. This is really important. It's unlikely that the meditation card will mean very much to you or that you'll drift into any relaxed state, unless you are fully focused on your breathing first. There is no substitute for breathing awareness and if you skip this phase, you will always end up disappointed. It would be rather like deciding you want a completely new career without having any form of training before you start work! To be aware of your breathing is the first and most important stage of entering meditation.

Now the first meditation card we're going to start with is the Word Card. This is the card shown opposite. First read through the exercise "Going into Words" and then prop up the Word Card in front of you. It doesn't matter which way up you place the Word Card. Close your eyes, go through your breathing awareness and then, when you feel ready, open your eyes and continue.

Word Card – Find this card at the back of the kit

GOING INTO WORDS

Open your eyes and look at the jumble of words. Relax. Take a nice, deep breath. One word will "jump" out at you, brighter or sharper than all the others. When this happens, acknowledge that this is the word you have chosen to meditate on at this time. Just let your gaze remain fixed on this word for a little while. Don't stare, just gaze gently at it.

THE MEDITATION KIT

You may find that your mind wants to take over and jump on to other words. You might suddenly feel as though perhaps you really ought to choose another one. Perhaps you don't like this word or you're unsure what it really means or you feel nervous about looking at its meaning. Just relax, breathe deeply, and realise this word is the right one for you. Do not change the word which first came to you.

Now you can either keep gazing at the word, or you may prefer to let your eyes close gently. You will find the word is still etched into your memory and you may even be able to see it in your mind's eye in front of you. If you feel the word is drifting away, open your eyes again and let your gaze fix upon the word for another period of time.

Say this word silently to yourself. Say it a number of times. Now ask yourself what this word means to you. Remember to keep breathing comfortably and deeply. It may even be a word that you don't know, but that doesn't matter at all. You are relaxing into deeper realms where mysteries can be solved. Just ask yourself what this word means. You may be given a straightforward reply, which seems logical, or you may find yourself surprised by the answer. Whatever answer you receive, question again, "What does this word really mean?" Does this word apply to your life? When have you experienced it or used this word? Is it a word that is lacking in your life? Why? What would you have to do to apply it?

Who do you know who personifies this word? How do they do it? Does this word make you feel emotional? Uplifted? Confused?

If you feel you are stuck with the word and can't work with it, return to your breathing and focus on that alone. Then pull the word back into your conscious thought and look at it again. Try not to strain too hard. Wallow in the word and its meaning. Let the word dance in and out of your conscious thought and play with it. Feel yourself floating on the word itself, flying upwards and outwards. Let your mind expand and enjoy what it is discovering.

Become playful with the word. Imagine the word is a long accordion that you pull in and out, or see it as a ball that you bounce up and down. Try throwing it out into nothingness and see what happens to the word when it is returned to you.

Try eating the word! What happens when it is digested by you? Wrap the word around your body. How does it feel? Does it seem to have a colour or feeling attached to it? Is it a particular texture, such as soft and warm or firm and strong? Keep playing with the experience and keep enjoying the freedom of what you are doing.

Here there are no boundaries. You can behave in whatever way feels appropriate to you and the word. Build up a

THE MEDITATION KIT

Imagine the words wrapped around your body

relationship and a rapport with the word and let yourself learn from the experience.

When you are ready, slowly withdraw from the word. Feel it float away into nothingness, or place it firmly back onto the Word Card again and withdraw it from your consciousness. This may take a few minutes to do. You can use your own technique to get rid of it. Use an imaginary tool to wipe it away or see the word as a light that is turned off. Have it fly up into infinity and slowly disappear. Say good-bye to the word in a way that suits you.

Now slowly open your eyes and focus on an object other than the Word Card in front of you. Take time to reorientate your thoughts. Bring yourself back to reality and give your body a little stretch. Take a few sips of your water. Notice how heavy your body feels but how relaxed it is also. Wait until you feel ready before you get up and continue with your everyday tasks.

How was that as a first experiment? You may have found it quite liberating and a great deal of fun. Or it may have been a profound and very moving experience. Perhaps you were frustrated and felt you couldn't work with the word. Whatever you discovered, it was absolutely right for you at this time. Everyone works in a different and very personal way with meditating.

Some people see vivid images. Others only sense things. Some people hear words of wisdom and want to listen. It's possible to sit in a state of emptiness and not get anything. Every experience is valid and personal to you. Meditation is a gentle, gradual process that shifts and alters as your own life changes. Don't try to compare your meditation sessions to anyone else's. Each will be individual. Just know that what is happening to you is exactly what is meant to happen. Enjoy the gentle discovery of it all.

Return to this Word Card on different occasions when you feel ready. You will discover different words jump out at you each time. Sometimes the same one will reappear because you have something more to learn from it. Keep placing the Word Card on different sides so that you see different words. Remember to be playful and keep experimenting with different actions whilst you are focusing on the word. On the next page there is a chart for you to keep your own personal record of what you discovered with different words.

Now we're going to move forward into the deeper realms of mantras and yantras. These are special words and symbols that have hidden meanings, used to achieve an even deeper state of relaxation and awareness. When you feel ready, we'll move on.

THE MEDITATION KIT

WORD CHART

Date	Word	What It Meant To Me

3. MANTRAS

The next meditation card we're going to work with is the Mantra Card. Mantras are basically words which resonate in a particular way inside of us and help us to go into a deeper state of relaxation. You may have found as you were working with the Word Card previously that some of the words were actually very soothing and pleasant to repeat over and over in your mind. You may have found yourself being lulled into a warm, comfortable feeling by the sing-song repetition of some of the words. If this happened to you, what you were experiencing was very much the sensation of a "mantra".

Usually, however, a mantra is not a proper word that we would recognise as English. This is because we want to focus on the calming rhythm of the sound, as opposed to becoming involved and side-tracked with the actual meaning of the word.

The mantra should be a warm and soothing sound. You can either say it out loud to yourself, repeating it constantly, slowly and rhythmically, or you can just think it quietly to yourself. Whatever you choose to do, it is a helpful means through which you can find yourself slipping into that deep state of calm, that inner sanctuary of stillness that we seek in meditation.

A word of warning here. Mantras can be extremely powerful. It is not until you try this for yourself that you understand how a simple sonorous sound constantly repeated really does affect both your mind and body. This is wonderful if you are ready for the

ME - NOM
RA - MA
SHUME
AH - SAM
LA - NAN
MA - RAH
SHA - LOON
VO - HUM

Mantra Card – Find this card at the back of the kit

strength of this experience and how it can transport you into new states of relaxation and awareness.

If at any time, you feel the power of this experience is too strong, simply stop. Let the mantra float away into nothingness and bring yourself back into your body by feeling how heavy your body is and by opening your eyes and focusing on a nearby object. You can always return to the mantras when you feel ready at a later stage. There is no rush. For others, it will be a more gentle process of gradually attaining a deeper level of awareness through repeated sound. Work at the level that is right for you.

Read through the following exercise ("Going into Mantras") first. Then prop the Mantra Card up in front of you and spend time focusing on your breathing before you continue.

GOING INTO MANTRAS

Open your eyes and gently focus on the words. This time you aren't going to wait for a word to jump out at you. Starting with the first word, say it out loud slowly three times. Remember to keep your breathing deep and comfortable. Take a breath in each time before you say the word and really feel it roll around and through you. Do you feel anything? It might be a tingle inside, a deep sense of calm or a tangible feeling of sinking pleasurably into a deeper state of relaxation. Now say the word silently to yourself and see what effect that has. Does it feel good?

If at any point, you feel uncomfortable or emotional, stop saying the word. Wash it away from your thoughts and then try another word. If at all the words feel too powerful for you, stop. Focus on your breathing and let yourself come back to reality gently and gradually.

If you are fine, then continue. Slowly work your way through the words. If at some point, you feel you have found the perfect word for you, still continue through the list. Let yourself fully experience each word. Go slowly and lose yourself fully in each word.

When you have reached the final word, then close your eyes again and focus on your breathing for a minute or two. Do you feel drawn to make up your own word now? Wait a minute and see if something comes to you. If it doesn't, that is fine. If it does, then slowly say the word out loud three times. How does it make you feel? Silently repeat it inside your head a number of times. Notice how it makes you feel.

When you are ready, withdraw from all the words you have practised. Open your eyes again and focus elsewhere for a while. Remember where you are and what you were doing before you started to meditate. Remember what else you have to do today. Take a drink of your water and then slowly stretch your limbs and wriggle your body. Make sure you feel ready to face the world again before you get up.

Some of you will have found that very powerful, perhaps too powerful at times. Others will have felt very little and wondered what all the fuss is about! Make a note of how you felt by filling in the chart opposite. Return to this Mantra Card on other occasions and see if time changes your experiences with the different sounds.

MANTRAS

MANTRA CHART

Date	Mantra	What I felt

If you do end up creating your own mantra, remember it's best to avoid using a real word. You want a sound into which you can literally "lose yourself". Sonorous sounds such as "n" and "m" are the most common because they have been shown to provide a soothing effect on the human body, although the gentle "sh" sound can also be very effective.

It's fine if you want to use one mantra for a period of time and then decide to change to another. Remember, our meditations change according to our needs. So it is quite natural that different mantras provide different benefits. Using the chart overleaf, keep a record of the mantras you end up using and notice how long you work with each mantra before changing it.

THE MEDITATION KIT

MY MANTRAS

Date (From – To)	Mantra	Changes I Felt With New Word

The mantras may have opened up a whole new world for you. If they have, feel free to use your word when you start each meditation. Always focus on your breathing first, and then start saying your mantra to yourself. Repeat it as many times as you feel is right, to help you sink into the state of relaxation and awareness, to help you find your own peaceful sanctuary. When you feel comfortable and ready, then withdraw from your mantra and continue with whatever Meditation Card you are working on. If you didn't feel any effect from the mantra or felt too strong an effect, you can always stop working with them for a while and then return at a later stage.

Now we're going to look at an equally fascinating but very different form of Meditation Card: Yantras.

4. YANTRAS

As mantras are sounds to help us achieve deeper states of meditation, yantras are visual aids to help us achieve greater awareness. Yantras are fundamentally geometric designs of ancient composition and they are deeply complex. Their true meanings reveal cosmic patterns of consciousness, unity and purpose. Don't worry if this is beginning to sound mysterious and very daunting. You are not about to try to become an expert in yantras and their deep meanings!

Your intention with working with these yantras is simply to enjoy their beautiful geometric patterns and to use the images as a means of relaxing further and further into a pleasant state which allows you to open your mind even more to other possibilities. If in that process you have some insight into life and its meaning on a deep level, that is a wonderful bonus! It is not what you are specifically setting out to do.

What is important for you to realise is that these are not just pretty designs that someone has drawn for fun. They represent an entire philosophy on the meaning of life. Yantras were created to demonstrate different powerful elements of existence, whether it be depicting male and female unity, the five elements of earth, fire, water, air and ether, the evolution of the cosmos or supreme symbols of protection, health and prosperity.

Despite their complexity or perhaps directly as a result of it, it is easy to lose yourself in these beautiful shapes and designs and to allow your mind to spiral onto other thoughts and levels of awareness.

It is helpful if you look at all the designs through a gentle, soft gaze. They are not meant to be intently stared at or analysed from a technical point of view. The more you blur your gaze and allow yourself to simply drift into the image, the more you are likely to get from it.

It's very possible that you will find some of these yantras much more evocative than others. One image may instantly send you spiralling off into a deep meditation whilst you may look at another for ages and wonder what on earth you are supposed to get from it! Whatever your initial response to a yantra card, remember to give yourself some time to relax into the image in front of you. Some will naturally take more work than others. Always, always remember to spend some time focusing on your breathing before you open your eyes and look at the card.

Now that we are working with the yantras, you might choose to change your process of meditating. Up until now, you have been reading through the exercise relating to each meditation card, before actually meditating upon the card. If you now feel confident and ready to try something different, why not prepare yourself as normal for meditation and then simply prop the appropriate card in front of you and meditate without reading through the exercise first? If nothing happens, or if you feel confused and uncertain, you can always return to reading through the exercise and use that to help your opening up and awareness. It would be a good experiment for you to see how your own free-thinking, meditative process is working.

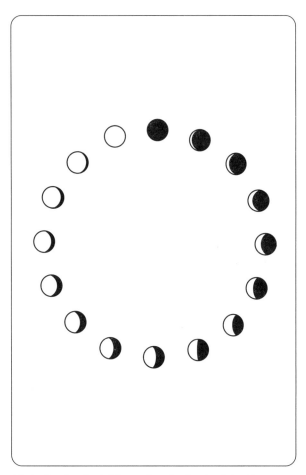

Circle Card – Find this card at the back of the kit

Whatever you experience through looking at a yantra card on your own, do then read through the exercise and do another meditation on the same card. Notice what changes occur as a result of your two different efforts.

When you work on your own, always remember to take your time to relax into the meditation. When you finish, always remember to withdraw yourself completely from the image. Wash it away using your own technique and let your eyes focus on another object to bring yourself back to reality again. Sip your water and take your time before you get up again.

We're going to start with what appears to be a simple design of a complete circle of small circles, going from black to white. Prop this Circle Card up in front of you, putting the completely black circle in the 12 o'clock position. Now prepare yourself to meditate upon it.

GOING INTO THE CIRCLE CARD

Let your gaze soften on the Circle Card and notice how the circles sweep around in a smooth arc, each section of light and dark gradually shifting. What in life represents this cycle? Think of all the different cycles that exist in the universe. Then think about different cycles in nature. Now allow yourself to focus on human beings and their different cycles. Realise, perhaps for the first time, how everything around us and in us is a circle of some sort. Spend some time acknowledging this fact. Allow your thoughts to spiral outwards and encompass bigger concepts. Keep looking at areas which manifest themselves as circles or cycles.

Now make the circle more personal and draw it into your own life. Where are you in your cycle of life? How does this make you feel? Now focus on different aspects of your own life. What are the elements that make up your life? How are they continuous and self-supporting? Are they unchangeable cycles or can you alter elements if you wish? What are the elements in your life that work for you? What would you like to change?

Which element of the circle are you drawn to? Do any of the circles seem more pleasing to you than others? Let your gaze be drawn to just one of the circles, if you wish, and focus on that. Feel yourself drawn into the one circle. What is it saying to you? How does it make you feel? Let your eyes drift to another circle and repeat the process. Go through each circle as an individual experience, if that feels right for you.

Then return to the circle as a whole. Soften your gaze and let the image blue in front of you. What is it saying to you now? Let yourself drift in that state of relaxation and awareness for as long as you like.

Why not play a game with the balls? Let the balls bounce around in your mind, feel them change position and jostle against each other. How does this make you feel? Freer? Less constrained? Enjoy the game. Let the circles have an energy of their own and see what happens. Enjoy the process.

Then, when you're ready, gradually pull yourself out of the meditation. Close your eyes, wash away the image, feel how heavy your body is and open your eyes. Now focus on another object.

Were you surprised by just how much a group of circles could end up meaning and what they made you think about? Perhaps you found yourself drifting off into other thoughts completely. It doesn't matter what happened, as long as you remained awake and mentally alert through the whole process. If you felt it wasn't a powerful image for you, remember to return to it on another occasion. Below is a chart for you to fill in when you're ready.

CIRCLE CARD CHART

Date	With/Without Exercise	Experience

CIRCLE CARD CHART

Date	With/Without Exercise	Experience

Now let's move on to the Figure Card. This is the only meditation card that has an outline of a seated figure. There is a design in the middle of the body. When you're ready, prop it up in front of you and begin.

GOING INTO THE FIGURE CARD

Settle and let yourself relax. Then open your eyes and focus on the Figure Card. Notice the figure is encased in a circle, relating to your previous experience with the Circle Card.

Take a moment to concentrate on the figure itself. Does this figure feel as though it relates to you? Does it relate to someone else you know? Does it refer to all of humanity as a whole? See what interpretation feels right for you during this meditation. Then see what the figure is saying to you. What does it mean? What do you need to learn from this image? Spend some time and let your thoughts drift into the figure itself. See what you can learn from it.

Figure Card – Find this card at the back of the kit

If you like, close your eyes and let the figure take on an energy and life of its own. Let it move about or dance in front of you. What is it saying to you? Feel its rejuvenating energy and enjoy the experience. When you are ready, have the figure sit back down again.

Then open your eyes again and refocus your gaze on the design within the body. Really gaze at the whole shape and see how it is made up of a series of complex designs. What do any of these symbols and images make you feel? Are you drawn to a particular part of the design or is it the whole which appeals to you? Try tuning in to just one section of the design and see what it is telling you. Notice if different parts make you feel differently. What do the interconnecting triangles make you feel? Focus on the black dot in the very middle and see what it says to you. What about the circle around these symbols? What about the petal shapes on the outside of the circle? Keep noticing how beautiful the design is and let yourself become lost within the various shapes. Notice how different parts of it jump out at you and then recede.

Now try to connect the figure and this complex design inside it. How are they connected? Or are they all part of a whole and completely inter-related? Can you see yourself in this figure? What would you have to do to be part of this complex design? Are you already a part of it? Lose yourself in the image and see how it makes you feel. Imagine pulling the central design into your own body and see how it makes you feel. Rest in that relaxed state for a moment. See what other insights come to you.

When you're ready, prepare to withdraw from the entire image. Perhaps you might want to thank the figure for entertaining you earlier and to let it know you will return again to enjoy its presence. Now let the whole image recede from your mind. Remember to give yourself enough time to refocus and reorientate yourself before you get up.

How did you find that as an experience? Remember to fill in the Figure Chart on the next page before the images and insights fade. It's best to write down your thoughts as soon as possible after you finish a meditation.

Don't worry if you find that you are having few experiences on your own and you need the exercise to help you to get started. It's also fine if you find some of the images difficult to work with. Just move on to the next meditation card when you're ready.

THE MEDITATION KIT

FIGURE CARD CHART

Date	With/Without Exercise	Experience

Now we're going to look at the Triangle Card. It is a series of inter-connecting triangles with one small white dot right in the centre. Place this in front of you and prepare to meditate.

GOING INTO THE TRIANGLE CARD

Start off by letting your gaze soften into the complex maze. Notice how it seems to pulse and move as your vision blurs over it. Let the image become like a 3-D form in front of you for a few minutes. How is this making you feel? What does it make you think of? Notice what sections seem to jump out at you and then let your gaze soften again so that another area comes into focus. Let yourself rest in this fluctuating state for a while and let your thoughts wash over you, without trying to consciously hold on to them.

Then let your gaze rest upon the white dot in the middle and let yourself be pulled into it. How does that make you feel? What is its significance in relation to the rest of the image?

Now pull your gaze back to encompass the whole image again. Notice how this is in fact a complex series of triangles, pointing upwards and downwards, suggesting some sort of inter-connecting duality in life. What does that make you think of? Where in the universe does this duality manifest itself?

YANTRAS

How is it inter-dependent? How important is it to the universe as a whole? Think of all the areas of duality in life and the universe and let your thoughts float through all the areas, noticing any insights that come up for you at this time.

When you are ready, withdraw from the image, using your cleansing and refocusing technique. Give yourself time to come back to reality.

Triangle card – Find this card at the back of the kit

Did you find your thoughts going into areas you hadn't thought about before? Have you almost forgotten already what some of those areas are? Fill in the Triangle Card Chart on the next page before you continue.

As you prepare to move on again, remember that it's fine if some of the meditation cards aren't meaning a great deal to you. You can always return to them again when you wish.

If you are having an easy time, with lots of relaxing imagery and sensations floating around and through you, that is wonderful. Continue with the next meditation card when you're ready. If you are feeling stuck in any way, why not return to your Window Card for a meditation and let your thought fly upwards and outwards again? It may be that you are straining too hard on the images and trying to make the experience too profound. Remember, meditation is meant to be fun and relaxing! Prop up your Window Card and let yourself fly away for a while. Continue when you feel ready.

THE MEDITATION KIT

TRIANGLE CARD CHART

Date	With/Without Exercise	Experience

The last yantra card we are going to work with looks somewhat like a snowflake with a star in the middle of it. Prop up this Star Card in front of you. Start when you're ready.

GOING INTO THE STAR CARD

Start by letting your eyes soften their focus. Let the image blur in front of you. Notice how it becomes like a 3-D image and let that dance in front of you. See how it pulsates and seems to change shape as you relax. Rest in this state for a while. Notice how sometimes the star seems to dominate and then it recedes as the surrounding design comes back into focus.

Realise there are also squares and triangles too. Bring them forward for a while and see how that makes you feel.

Now let yourself sink down into the middle and go into the star itself. How do you feel now? What images or sensations wash over you? Realise that there is a further black dot within the centre of this star. Sink down yet further into its wonderful, inky warmth. Relax. Rest there for a period of time and see what washes over you. When you are ready, pull your focus back to the outer design.

When you're ready, pull back again and see the image as a whole. How is the star connected to the surrounding design? How does the whole design resonate within you now? Wallow in the sensation. Take your time.

Then slowly wash away the image. Close your eyes and feel it disappear using your own technique. Focus on you and your own body now and how it feels. Take time to reorientate yourself. Have a sip of water.

Remember to fill in the Star Card Chart on the next page as soon as possible.

Do you feel somewhat floaty after all the meditations? Remember to make sure you are back in reality again before you continue your daily tasks.

Did you find all four images very different? Did each one leave you feeling differently? Each of the four yantras was designed for different elements of universal awareness. The contents of some of the exercises hinted at these intentions but it is up to you to form your own personal conclusions as to how you felt about each. As meditation is such an intensely personal journey, it is better that you experience each meditation card in your own way as it then becomes deeply meaningful to you.

Star card – Find this card at the back of the kit

Now take a walk over the crinkly edges surrounding the star. What does it feel like? Walk in different directions. Stop and see what sensations come to you. Explore the surface and feel its texture. What are the indecipherable markings in each area? Notice how they are all different. What might they all mean? Linger over different areas and see how they make you feel.

THE MEDITATION KIT

STAR CARD CHART

Date	With/Without Exercise	Experience

If, at some point in the future, you really want to know more about what is intended behind these four yantras, there is a brief description of their individual meanings at the back of this book. You may find these confusing. The meaning of a yantra is not simple or necessarily easy to grasp at first. However, as was said earlier, you do not have to become experts on yantras to enjoy them!

This is why it is advisable not to read the yantra meanings until you have spent some time meditating on the yantras first. It is then interesting to go back and repeat the meditations all over again, and notice what this new knowledge does to your meditating process. Sometimes it may enhance what you have already discovered; at other times it may seem the entire meditation goes down a different path and it feels as though you are looking at a completely new meditation card. Give yourself plenty of time before you skip forward and read the yantras' meanings.

Now we're going to look at the form other meditations might take and how they could benefit you in different areas of your life. So let's now take a step into your future and see what meditation might look like there!

5. THE FUTURE

So how have you felt through your various meditations so far? Have you generally felt more relaxed and calmer as a result? If you have fallen asleep through some of them, don't worry! That is a normal state in the early days. If it keeps happening, try not to meditate at a time when you are particularly tired. Give yourself some extra sleep time at night if you know you are really over-tired. Meditation is a wonderfully regenerative action but sleep is also extremely important. The usual reason you fall asleep during meditation is simply because you are lacking those extra hours of sleep. One cannot replace the other.

Everyone goes through different phases along their personal path of meditation. Some days you may find it harder than usual to relax and to retreat into your sanctuary. On other days, you may find yourself going into the deepest relaxation without consciously putting much effort into it.

Although the ideal is to lose yourself in each meditation so that physically you are completely still, sometimes this feels impossible. It's usual to go through a stage where you feel physically uncomfortable and long to wriggle about and stretch out your muscles. You may have a phase where you keep developing new itches during meditation and find that they seem to dominate your thoughts!

There are different schools of thought about wanting to scratch during meditation. As the intention is to remain motionless, meditators are often told to ignore any irritating sensation, to focus purely on their breathing and it will then disappear. Sometimes this does work.

However, it's also possible to reach a point where it seems as though the itching is monopolising every thought in your head. You could then try adopting this attitude: let it! Focus all your thoughts on the part of you which is itching and instead of physically moving to rub it, just think intently about how it itches. Repeat the word "itchy" to yourself, over and over again if necessary. Focus on the spot concerned. The fascinating aspect of this is that often the total focus alone is enough to stop the irritation, without you touching it! It's something you need to experience for yourself to prove that it can work.

Whatever phase you find yourself in, acknowledge it is simply that – a phase. Your meditations will grow and change, reflecting the changes in your own personal life. Whatever is happening to you, it is the right experience for you to have at this given moment in your life.

So how often is it suggested that you meditate? You will notice no reference has been made so far about frequency of meditations.

The ideal is to find a little time each day in which to stop and relax. You will have realised by now that however enjoyable other relaxing hobbies may be, such as reading or watching

THE MEDITATION KIT

television or going out with friends, meditation comes into an entirely different realm. You cannot compare the sense of peace and relaxation that comes over you from having spent a little time meditating.

The secret is not to think of it as a lengthy period each day. If you really can spare only ten minutes a day, or even five minutes, that is still far better than none at all. By allowing yourself just a few minutes each day, you create the possibility of gradually increasing the length of time as and when you can. Regular, short meditations are just as powerful, if not more powerful, than very infrequent bursts of intense meditation. Also try to get into the habit of taking mini-meditations through the day. This is the sort mentioned earlier where you close your eyes for a minute and focus on your breath. Feel the tension ebbing out of you when you do this.

It's important for you to realise that although the meditation cards offered here really are your gateway into a new world, they are also just a sample of what is available for you. You might want to consider focusing on other objects and see how they make you feel.

So what might these other objects be? What constitutes a suitable focus for meditation? Do you love flowers and plants? Put a single rose in front of you and use that as a focus for your meditation. Perhaps you have tried working with a candle and found that

helpful. You may have a favourite crystal or a piece of beautiful driftwood that you want to use. Are you particularly fond of a painting or poster and you know that you can literally "lose yourself" into it? Experiment with what is around you and see what else works for you. Periodically, return to all the meditation cards and see what new experiences come up for you. Realise that you can use meditation in many ways.

Do you often have issues that come up and you aren't sure how to deal with them? Give yourself a little time to meditate. Go into that wonderful, warm state of relaxation, into your inner sanctuary and silently ask yourself what you can do to sort out a problem or worry. Did you find the figure on the Figure Card helpful when you were meditating? Prop up the Figure Card in front of you again and ask for help. You may be amazed at the guidance and nurturing that you are given.

Do you find that looking at the Window Card really helps you to retreat quickly into your wonderfully private sanctuary of peace and stillness? Perhaps you feel that this sanctuary of calm is still eluding you. Sometimes, people feel more confident if they actually create a beautiful place in their mind's eye and they then use this focus as a means of entering a deeply relaxed state.

So, to help you in this process, let's look at a guided meditation that doesn't use a meditation card initially. For this, it's best if you enlist the help of a friend who is sympathetic to meditation.

THE FUTURE

Perhaps they already meditate themselves. If not, it may be a good time to suggest it to them! If you don't know anyone suitable, you can always read the exercise below and then close your eyes and go through it, remembering what you can for yourself. It is often easier, however, if you can listen to a gentle voice saying the words out loud. If someone is speaking this out loud, ask them if they can speak softly and quite slowly. Every "..." indicates a place where the person might like to pause for a moment or two before continuing.

SPOKEN MEDITATION

Settle comfortably into your favourite meditation chair and wriggle your body gently to relax your muscles. Close your eyes. Give yourself a moment to do nothing but focus on yourself... Feel the tension slipping away from you...

Now bring your attention to your breathing. Let yourself become aware of each breath as it comes through your nostrils. Watch each breath as you exhale. Stay in this comfortable state for some time... Feel how your breath deepens and becomes slower without your having to make any effort... Remember to keep your eyes closed. Relax...

Now you are walking through a beautiful garden. It is warm and the sun is shining. There is a clear blue sky above you. Around you are wonderful flowers, plants and trees. The grass under your feet feels soft and warm. Birds are singing.

There is a gentle, warm breeze blowing... Picture this beautiful garden and wander around it, enjoying every part of it... Take your time...

As you walk through this beautiful garden, you see a gate ahead of you. You are curious. You walk up to the gate and open it. As you close it behind you, you realise that in front of you is a beautiful building. This is your dream building. It is whatever shape and size you choose. It is exactly what you want it to be. Give yourself time to see it clearly in front of you... See its colour... See its shape... See its texture... It is shimmering gently in the sunlight.

As you approach it, you notice that there is a door into this wonderful building. Now you see that there is a handle on this door. Gently open it and walk inside.

You are now in a beautiful room shimmering with iridescent light. You feel safe, secure, utterly protected. The room is warm and bright. It is your perfect room. Take your time and create its colour... texture... size... shape... Feel completely at one with your room and its decor...

Now you are going to sit in the centre of the room and let yourself be still for a while. You soak in the nurturing rays of gentle light around you and enjoy your sense of peace... Let yourself sink contentedly into deep, velvet silence... Into

43

THE MEDITATION KIT

stillness... Realise that you have at last found the inner core of you... You are now completely at peace... Everything is perfect. Everything is exactly as it ought to be... Rest in this deep relaxation for some time...

When you are ready, slowly get up and walk back to the door. When you get to the door, you turn and look back at this beautiful room for one last time. Now you notice that in the centre of the room, there is a present for you. This is personal to you. Pick it up and take it with you. This is a gift just for you.

Now slowly leave the building, closing the door behind you. Walk back to the garden gate and go through it, closing the gate behind you... You are back in your glorious garden again. Walk back down the path, noticing how fresh and lovely everything is and how wonderful it all smells...

Now you are going to leave the garden and your sanctuary behind. You can always return to this space at any time but right now, it is time for you to say good-bye... You are now back in this room. You are sitting in your chair... Realise how heavy your body now feels in the chair... Think about what day of the week it is and what time it is now... When you are ready, open your eyes... Focus on an object and make sure you are back in reality again. Wait a few minutes before you speak. Take your time...

Did you find that an enjoyable experience? Were you surprised at the gift that was left for you? Think about what it means to you and how significant it is for you right now. You can take this trip again whenever you wish. Once you are familiar with it, you can take the journey on your own and you won't need anyone to talk you through it.

Were you struck by how vivid the garden was and how beautiful everything was? Did the building seem physically real to you? Did you feel as though you knew the room as soon as you entered it? You will see that there are three blank cards in this kit. They are for you to decorate as you wish. Put on them whatever you find inspirational for meditating.

If you are good at drawing, why not draw the garden or building you created during your last meditation on one of the blank cards? Don't worry if drawing isn't one of your strengths. Look through magazines and see what you feel drawn to. Put on the blank cards whatever you would like to use as a focus to take you into your private sanctuary.

You might find your thoughts going a different way. Perhaps you'd like another meditative image, such as an animal, a protective symbol or a single flower that you find inspirational. Perhaps you have a dried flower and find that beautiful. Draw or place whatever you want onto these blank cards. Make it personal for you. This is your gateway into freedom.

THE FUTURE

Experiment with drawing your own cards

THE MEDITATION KIT

Now let's look at one last issue before we finish. Have you had any sensation of someone or something being there for you during any of your meditations?

This could take any form. You might have found the figure in the Figure Card helpful. Perhaps your image came in the form of a beautiful animal. Perhaps you had a spiritual experience with someone personal to you appearing to comfort or to guide you. You might just sense someone or something with you without seeing anything. Perhaps you feel that what you do in meditation is simply to work with aspects of your own self and that you are learning to access a deeper part of you.

Whatever is "real" for you, it is important to acknowledge and appreciate help in whatever form it takes. Acknowledgement and appreciation help to strengthen the "relationships" you create in your meditations. This is true whether it relates to an outside energy or to your own self. So we are going to close with a suggested offering of thanks for the guidance and nurturing we receive during meditation. You might choose to say this silently as you finish meditating. You may want to make up your own private "thank you" which feels right for you.

Remember, whatever you do, continue to enjoy your meditations as a regular and pleasurable part of your everyday life. Make sure you are gentle with yourself and allow your meditations to nurture and inspire your own personal journey in life.

A THANK YOU

Thank you for your loving presence and nurturing guidance during my meditations.

Please continue to help me along my own personal path of

progress until we are able to meet again.

THE CIRCLE YANTRA

This yantra basically contains the elements of delight and is a celebration of existence as a whole. Meditation on this is to bring good fortune, dispel fears and bring enjoyment to the meditator. Thus it is also used for wish-fulfilment.

These cycles of the moon each represent different areas. Starting with the black circle (dark night), each circle signifies the following states:

• fulfilling desires

• charming and inciting opportunities to arise

• granting fortune and supernatural powers

• freedom from all evil influences

• mastery of the forces of nature

• destroying cruelty

• destroying fear and bestowing prosperity and one's desires

• granting beauty and fame and expanding learning processes

• bestowing esoteric knowledge

• becoming beneficent

• mastery over evil forces in nature

• conquests and prosperity

• total beneficence

• obtaining knowledge of one's previous births

• granting the object of one's desires

The last circle is a representation of the full moon.

THE FIGURE YANTRA

The figure shows a human form in meditative posture symbolising awareness of such a state.

The central square is an extremely complex composition of geometric designs. Put into very broad terms, this shows a 9 circuit path which leads the meditator into the enlightened state necessary to understand cosmic laws. For instance, the dot in the centre represents the sacred state of the cosmos, while the outside circle represents the strength and power of the whole universe. All the other sections in between are symbols of how the meditator can invoke different Mantras and thought processes in order to achieve enlightenment.

This yantra as a whole signifies the human psyche achieving true unity with the universe. It demonstrates that this happens through the ritual of meditating and chanting which alters the human state and transports it onto a level of universal understanding.